SCRIBBLED
IN THE DARK

SCRIBBLED IN THE DARK

POEMS

CHARLES SIMIC

ecco

An Imprint of HarperCollinsPublishers

HarperCollins books may be purchased for educational, business, or sales promotional use. For information, please e-mail the Special Markets Department at SPsales@harpercollins.com.

A hardcover edition of this book was published in 2017 by Ecco, an imprint of HarperCollins Publishers.

FIRST ECCO PAPERBACK EDITION PUBLISHED 2018.

Designed by Suet Yee Chong

Library of Congress Cataloging-in-Publication Data has been applied for.

ISBN 978-0-06-266118-0

18 19 20 21 22   LSC   10 9 8 7 6 5 4 3 2 1

FOR HELEN

It's not as though I had a cow to milk,
or do I?

—*James Tate*

CONTENTS

I

II

III

IV

ACKNOWLEDGMENTS

These poems were first published in the following magazines, to whose editors grateful acknowledgment is made: *The New Yorker, The Paris Review, The New York Review of Books, Boulevard, London Review of Books, Tin House, The Nation, Boston Review, Monkey Business, The Threepenny Review, A Public Space,* and the *New York Times Magazine.*

SCRIBBLED
IN THE DARK

DARK NIGHT'S FLY CATCHER

Thatched myself
Over with words.

Night after night
Thatched myself

Anew against
The pending eraser.

SEEING THINGS

I came here in my youth,
A wind toy on a string.
Saw a street in hell and one in paradise.
Saw a room with a light in it so ailing
It could've been leaning on a cane.
Saw an old man in a tailor shop
Kneel before a bride with pins between his lips.
Saw the President swear on the Bible
    while snow fell around him.
Saw a pair of lovers kiss in an empty church
And a naked man run out of a building
    waving a gun and sobbing.
Saw kids wearing Halloween masks
Jump from one roof to another at sunset.
Saw a van full of stray dogs look back at me.
Saw a homeless woman berating God
And a blind man with a guitar singing:
"Oh Lord remember me,
When these chains are broken set my body free."

AT THE VACANCY SIGN

There was a small room in the back
With a bed and a chair,
And a grim old woman
Who unlocked the door
And made herself scarce,
Leaving you there alone
With a thin ray of sunlight
You could imagine talking to
Every time it dropped in for a visit,
And falling quiet
As it got ready to leave.

THAT ELUSIVE SOMETHING

Was it in the smell of freshly baked bread
That came to greet you out of the bakery?
The sight of two girls playing with dolls
On the steps of a building blackened by fire?

In this city you might've seen once
In a dream or knew in another life,
This street calm as a sharpshooter
Taking his aim in the bright sunlight,

Perhaps at that woman turning a corner,
Pushing a baby carriage ahead of her,
You ran after, as if the child in it was you,
And found yourself lost afterwards

In a crowd of strangers, feeling like someone
Stepping out after a long illness
Who can't help but see the world with his heart
And hopes not to forget what he saw.

FAIR-WEATHER FRIENDS

Eddie with flowing locks, plus Joey and me,
Like Jesus and two thieves
Crucified side by side on the blackboard,
Our backs slumped in defeat
While awaiting our punishment.

The Lord took pity on them, wiped
Their souls clean with a sponge.
Not mine. I remained where I was
Holding on to a piece of chalk
Long after they had all gone home.

Night already fallen everywhere,
Hard to be sure what numbers
Still remain there to be added
Or subtracted or whether someone
Is watching as I give them a last try.

UNINVITED GUEST

Dark thought on a sunny day
Languid miss in distress
Everyone's blind date
With a look of having a secret
Knife drawer in a madman's kitchen
A crow flying round my head
Suicide's friend
Soft-footed gravedigger of our hopes
Hell's night nurse
Bending over a cradle.

ALL GONE INTO THE DARK

Where's that blind street preacher who said
The world will end Thursday at noon?
Or that woman who walked down Madison
Stark naked and holding her head high?

Where's the poet Delmore Schwartz
Arguing with a ghost on a park bench?
Where's the drunk young man on crutches
Wanting to kill more Vietnamese?

Mr. Undertaker, savoring a buttered roll
In a window of a coffee shop, you ought to know—
Or are you, like the rest of us, in the dark
As you make ready to bury another stiff?

THE WEEK

Monday comes around with a new tattoo
It won't show us and here's Tuesday
Walking its latest nightmare on a leash
And Wednesday blind as the rain tapping
On a windowpane and Thursday sipping
Bad coffee served by a pretty waitress
And Friday lost in a confusion of sad
And happy faces and Saturday flashing
Like a pinball machine in the morgue
And Sunday with a head of crucified Christ
Hanging sideways in a bathroom mirror

TO BOREDOM

I'm the child of rainy Sundays.
I watched time crawl
Like an injured fly
Over the wet windowpane.
Or waited for a branch
On a tree to stop shaking,
While Grandmother knitted
Making a ball of yarn
Roll over like a kitten at her feet.
I knew every clock in the house
Had stopped ticking
And that this day will last forever.

FISH OUT OF WATER

That's what you always were, my friend.
Just the other day
A stuffed parrot perched
In splendor of an antiques store,
Gave you a dirty look
As you stuck your nose in.

Like running into a mirror
One night crossing a vast
And empty shopping mall
With an odd-looking stranger
Cooling his heels in it
Surprised to find you there.

Or driving past a scarecrow
Someone relocated
To a graveyard near your home
And hearing his laughter
Long after you went back the next day
And found him gone.

ILLEGIBLE SCRIBBLE

These rags the spirit borrows
To clothe itself
Against the chill of mortality.
O barbed wire of crossed-out words,
Crown of thorns,
Camp meeting of dead wall reveries,
Spilled worry beads,
Fortune-teller's coffee dregs,
My footholds in the abyss.

HISTORY

Our life stories are scary and droll,
Like masks children wear on Halloween
As they go from door to door
Holding the little ones by the hand
In some neighborhood long torn down,

Where people ate their dinners
In angry silence or quarreling loudly,
When there was a knock on the door,
A soft knock a shy boy makes
Dressed in a costume his mother made.

What's this you're wearing, kid?
And where did you get that mask?
That made everyone laugh here
While you stood staring at us,
As if you knew already we were history.

SIGNS OF THE TIMES

For a mind full of disquiet
A trembling roadside weed is Cassandra,
And so is the sight
Of a boarded up public library,
The rows of books beyond its windows
Unopened for years,
The sickly old dog on its steps,
And a man slumped next to him,
His mouth working mutely
Like an actor unable to recall his lines
At the end of some tragic farce.

IN THE COURTROOM

The judge appears to be asleep:
His heavy eyelids are lowered
And his black glasses rest
On a thick stack of documents.

Take your shoes off as you enter,
So as not to disturb his rest,
But keep your white socks on.
The floor of the courtroom is cold.

What's left of the fading daylight
Is about to make its quiet exit,
Leaving the darkness in our souls
To do what it damn pleases here.

MISSED CHANCE

One afternoon looking for a shortcut,
I found myself on a street
That I'd never known was there,
And might've gone no further—
With my foot arrested in midstride

Before a dogwood tree in flower,
Towering in someone's yard
And a few brightly colored toys
Scattered along their driveway,
But no child or anyone else in sight.

One caged bird chirping in a window
Who may've been in on the secret?
I didn't wait to find out, but hurried away
Wherever it seemed more important
For me to show my face that day.

JANUARY

Children's fingerprints
On a frozen window
Of a small schoolhouse.

An empire, I read somewhere,
Maintains itself through
The cruelty of its prisons.

IN WONDER

I cursed someone or something
Tossing and turning all night—
Or so I was told, though I had no memory
Who it could be, so I stared
At the world out there in wonder.
The frost lay pretty on the bushes
Like tinsel over a Christmas tree,
When a limo as long as a hearse
Crept into view stopping at each
Mailbox as if in search of a name,
And not finding it sped away,
Its tires squealing like a piglet
Lifted into the air by a butcher.

IN THE SNOW

Tracks of someone lost,
Bleakly preoccupied,
Meandering blindly
In these here woods,

Licking his wounds
And crunching the snow,
As he trudges on,
Bereft and baffled,

In mounting terror
With no way out,
Jinxed at every turn,
A mystery to himself.

ANCIENT COMBATANT

Veteran of foreign wars,
Stiff in arm and leg,
His baggy pants billowing in the wind
Salutes a crow in a tree,

And resumes his stroll
Past a small graveyard,
Swerving and waving his arms
As if besieged by ghosts

Lurking among headstones,
Waiting to accost him
And make a clean breast
Before he slips out of sight.

The tiger lilies bemused.
The curving dirt road in his wake
Deep in silence
And prey to lengthening shadows.

THE NIGHT AND THE COLD

Torturers with happy faces,
You've made a prisoner strip naked
And stand strung with electric wires
Like a Christmas tree
In a department store window
Next to a smiling family gathered
Around a fake brick fireplace.

And as for you, men and women
Sprawled in dark doorways,
Along this street I'm walking,
Stuff your clothes with more newspaper,
The night will be long and cold.

ALL THINGS IN PRECIPITOUS DECLINE

Like a pickup with its wheels gone,
And some rusty and disassembled
Antique stoves and refrigerators
In a front yard choked with weeds,
Outside a shack with a plastic sheet
Draped over one of its windows,
Where a beer bottle went through
One star-studded night in June—
Or was it a shotgun we heard?
The police inquiry, if there is one,
Is proceeding at a snail's pace,
In the meantime, the old recluse
Got himself a bad-tempered mutt
To keep his junk company and bark
At all comers, including the mailman
Leaving a rare letter in the mailbox.

THE CRICKET ON MY PILLOW

His emaciated head and legs
Speak of long fasts, frantic prayers,

Dark nights of the soul,
And other unknown torments,

Before he found refuge in our home
From that madman out there

Who threw over his bed
A heavy blanket of snow.

WINTER FLY

You ought to live in a palace like a king
And not shiver on my kitchen wall,
Have a bed and chair made to measure
And a radio playing the latest hits
The flies in Dakar and Rio are humming,
While servants serve you pastries
On plates bearing your coat of arms,
And your courtiers look to catch you
A lady companion from among the flies
Grooming themselves on a dead dog.

BARE TREES

They are fans of horror film
In the fading light of a November day,
The gray surface of the pond
Is a movie screen they are watching.

The bare branches moving in it,
Are like the fingers of the blind
Reaching to touch the face of someone
Who'd been calling out to them

In the voice of geese flying over,
The shots of a hunting rifle,
And a dog barking outside a trailer
For someone to hurry and let him in.

ROADHOUSE

The news of the world is always old.
Nothing new ever happens,
The innocent get slaughtered
While some guy on TV makes excuses,

And the bartender refills our drinks,
His left hand clasped behind
His arching back, either maimed
By a dog or wielding a blackjack.

Our wars, it seems, are not going well.
A senator got caught soliciting sex
In a public bathroom at an airport,
And rain and snow are on the way.

STRAY HEN

The hounds of hell are barking again,
Better look for a tree to climb,
Befriend a rat slipping into a sewer,
The kite someone set free in the sky.

The watermelons we saw last summer
Falling out of a truck and breaking
Into bloody chunks on the highway,
May have already foretold our story.

Stray hen, is what they call our neighbor,
The one always looking lost,
Always clucking about something
And crossing herself as if she were in church.

I fear she hears those hounds barking,
And so does that man I see every night
In the picture window of his home
Sitting with a lit candle at a long table.

THE WHITE CAT

Mother was beginning to worry about me.
Moping around, still unmarried,
Destined to sit in the same gray sweater
And the same chair for the rest of my life,
Playing with the same three buttons.

I bought her a radio to cheer her up.
Even dance music sounded sad to her.
The quiet was better, especially on Sundays.
Together we'd watch the rain fall,
The night come, weary of being night,
And having to turn up at the appointed hour
Wearing the same black garments.

The buildings across the street were dark
While the sky had suddenly cleared.
I thought I heard Mother call my name,
So I covered my ears with my hands
And watched a white cat with its tail raised,
Walking cautiously along the parapet,
Stop and take a peek in every window.

THE ONE WHO DISAPPEARED

Now that it's warm enough to sit on the porch at night
Someone happened to remember a neighbor,
Though it had been more than thirty years
Since she went for a little walk after dinner
And never came back to her husband and children.

No one present could recall much about her,
Except how she'd smile and grow thoughtful
All of a sudden and would not say what about,
When asked, as if she already had a secret,
Or was heartbroken that she didn't have one.

THE MESSAGE

Take a message, crow, as the day breaks.
And find the one I hold dear,
Tell her the trees are almost bare
And the nights here are dark and cold.

Learn if she lights the stove already,
Goes to bed naked or fully dressed,
Sips hot tea in the morning, watching
Neighbors' children wait for a school bus.

Tell her nothing fills me with more sorrow,
Than the memory of seeing her
Covering her face with her hands
When she thought she was alone.

Help me, bird, flapping from tree to tree
And calling in a voice full of distress,
To some fond companion of yours
You'd like to see flying by your side.

BIRDS KNOW

There's a pond, a man said,
Far back in these woods,
Birds and deer know about
And slake their thirst there

In a water so cold and clear,
It's like a brand-new mirror
No one had a chance to look at,
Save, perhaps, that little boy,

Who went missing years ago,
And may've drowned in it,
Or left some trace of himself
Playing along its rocky edges.

I better go and find out,
This very night, I said to myself,
With my mind running wild,
And the moon out there so bright.

III

THE MOVIE

My childhood, an old silent movie.
O, winter evenings
When Mother led me by the hand
Into a darkened theater
Where a film had already started—
Like someone else's dream
Into which we happened to drop in—

With a young woman writing a letter
And pausing to wipe her eyes
In a room looking out on some harbor
And a bird sitting quietly in her cage,
No one was paying any attention to,
Nor to the white ship on the horizon,
Perhaps drawing closer, perhaps sailing away.

It was an occupied city, I forgot to say.
We trudged our way home
Bundled up heavily against the cold,
Keeping our eyes to the ground
Along the treacherous, dimly lit streets.

BELLADONNA

A word that comes to mind tonight
Strolling past red paper lanterns,
Bead curtains, and Oriental carpets
In a softly lit window of a fortune-teller.

A pretty girl in white evening gown
Seated at a small round table
Awaiting the arrival of the oracle
With tears streaking down her face.

A sight the live parrot on the premises
May want to comment on from his perch,
And the devil himself display tonight
To a young monk kneeling in prayer.

ON CLOUD NINE

Most days I'm airborne.
Nights too.
One foot before the other
On a thread so thin
A spider couldn't tell it from its own,
I promenade unseen
Over your heads.
You who are always ready
To applaud a fireman
Saving a child from a burning building,
Look up now and then
And try to catch my act.

SWEPT AWAY

Melville had the sea and Poe his nightmares,
To thrill them and haunt them,
And you have the faces of strangers,
Glimpsed once and never again.

Like that woman whose eye you caught
On a crowded street in New York
Who spun around after she went by
As if she had just seen a ghost.

Leaving you with a memory of her hand
Rising to touch her flustered face
And muffle what might've been something
She was saying as she was swept away.

MY GODDESS

Your nose is red, your eyes tear,
And you have sniffles
As if you've been watching
Soap operas all afternoon.

Diane—or whatever you call yourself—
Unless I can get you a drink
You may catch a bad cold
And have to stay in bed for a week.

Dearest, it's true you deserve
Far better than this rotgut
I found under the kitchen sink.
Still, go ahead and take a swig,

And stop pestering me to order
Chinese food at this hour
And find you a pair of dark glasses
You could wear in bed for me.

THE LUCKY COUPLE

This warm spring weather made them lazy
Sitting side by side on a park bench
With eyes closed and sunlight on their faces,
Listening to children in the playground
And some bird chirping in the trees
Long after they should've been back in the office.

One of them ought to have had the sense
To peek at their watch and with a shout
Drag the other away by the arm.
His excuse is, he's with a beautiful woman
Incapable of lifting a finger to save them
From being both sacked upon their return.

For now, with their legs stretched out
And their arms folded, they are content.
The people hurrying by must think
How lucky these two must be without
A care in the world, unlike that bunch
Looking pissed as they exit the courthouse.

DEAD SURE

Lovebirds smooching in the street,
The end of the world is coming.
Even that legless veteran
Asking schoolgirls for some change
Is going to hell in a hurry,
Because he keeps using
The name of our Lord in vain.
The old man holding the sign
With a grim look on his face
Is sure he'll be the one saved.

THE LOVER

When I lived on a farm I wrote love letters
To chickens pecking in the yard,
Or I'd sit in the outhouse writing one to a spider
Mending his web over my head.
That's when my wife took off with the mailman.
The neighbors were leaving, too.
Their sow and piglets squealing
As they ran after the moving truck,
And even that scarecrow I once tied to a tree
So it would have to listen to me.

THE SAINT

The woman I love is a saint
Who deserves to have
People falling on their knees
Before her in the street
Asking for her blessing.
Instead, here she is on the floor,
Hitting a mouse with a shoe
As tears run down her face.

THE ART OF HAPPINESS

Thanks to a stash of theatrical costumes
And their kindly owner,
An opportunity for this couple to brighten up
This dark and dreary day,

Cut a dash as they step out
Into the crowded street
Wearing powdered wigs,
Cross against the screeching traffic,
And go have lunch,
She looking like Marie Antoinette,
And he all in black,
Like her executioner or father confessor,

Watching the young French Queen
Splashing ketchup over her fries
With a wicked smile on her face,
While he struggles to balance the straw
That came with the Coke
On his nose and waits for her applause.

IN SOMEONE'S BACKYARD

What a pretty sight
To see two lovers drink wine and kiss,
A dog on his hind legs
Begging for table scraps.

CHERRY PIE

If it's true that the devil has his finger
In every pie, he must be waiting
For the night to fall, the darkness to
Thicken in the yard, so we won't see him
Lick the finger he dipped in your pie,
The one you took out of the oven, love,
And left to cool by the open window.

A DAY CAME

The birdcage was gone and the couch
With your parents on it watching TV.
Nor did we notice the moving truck,
The driver waving to us as he drove away.

I like the new look of our lives, you said,
Dangling a beer bottle by the neck
And walking pleased from room to room,
Every one of which was now empty.

Stepping out at last to look for our car,
We found neighbors' homes trashed,
Their front lawns covered with weeds
A few of which had pretty blue flowers

That seemed pleased to be there,
As crows do finding a roadkill.
The interests of certain powerful parties
In this country were being met.

Would that include God? I wondered
While you lay next to me on the floor,
Dead to the world. Still, you'd expect
Someone that big to lift a finger.

HAUNTED HOUSE

When the evening silence that lingered
Under a tree listening to a bird,
Strolls over to the village church
And then waits on its stone steps
For the minister to come and let it in—

But no one's about, either in the church
Or in the row of stately homes,
Each one of them long unoccupied
And kept in good order by their ghosts,
Like the one that struck a match,

When the power went out last night
And a woman as nature made her
Could be seen descending the stairs
Carrying one lit candle and climbing
Afterwards with a slice of watermelon.

THE BLIZZARD

O to be inside a mailbox
On a snow-piled street corner
Snuggled against a letter
Sending love and hot kisses
To some lucky fellow out there.

IV

THE INFINITE

The infinite yawns and keeps yawning.
Is it sleepy?
Does it miss Pythagoras?
The sails on Columbus's three ships?
Does the sound of the surf remind it of itself?
Does it ever sit over a glass of wine
    and philosophize?
Does it peek into mirrors at night?
Does it have a suitcase full of souvenirs
    stashed away somewhere?
Does it like to lie in a hammock with the wind
    whispering sweet nothings in its ear?
Does it enter empty churches and light a single
    candle on the altar?
Does it see us as a couple of fireflies
    playing hide-and-seek in a graveyard?
Does it find us good to eat?

LAST BET FOR THE NIGHT

Wagered one more thought
Against the universe,
The one about this moment
I'm living through
Being all that's true,
With my heart leaping
To place another red chip
On this dark night's
Vast and unattended gaming table.

DESCRIPTION

It was like a teetering house of cards,
A contortionist strumming a ukulele,
A gorilla raging in someone's attic,
A car graveyard frantic to get back
On the highway in a tornado,
Tolstoy's beard in his mad old age,
General Custer's stuffed horse . . .
What was? I ask myself and have no idea,
But it'll come to me one of these days.

MYSTERY THEATER

Bald man smoking in bed,
Naked lightbulb over his head,

The shadow of his cigar
Next to him on the wall,

Its long ash about to fall
Into a pitch-dark fishbowl.

SHADOW ON THE WALL

Round midnight,
Let's invite
A fellow bedlamite
For a bite.

LOOKING FOR A PLACE TO HIDE

I went down the street of false gods
The street of men dressed to kill
The street of a rat breaking cover
The street of moths courting and mating at night
The street of runaway brides

The street of the grand hotel on the skids
The street of painted smiles
The street of the sorcerer's apprentice
The street of smoke and mirrors
The street of shadow puppets

The street of bloody wars and revolutions
The street of the pacing tiger
The street of a policeman on his horse
The street of a sleepwalking child
The street of the illegible address

SCRIBBLED IN THE DARK

A shout in the street.
Someone locking horns with his demon.
Then, calm returning.
The wind tousling the leaves.
The birds in their nests
Pleased to be rocked back to sleep.
Night turning cool.
Streams of blood in the gutter
Waiting for sunrise.

IN THE GREEK CHURCH

The holy icon of the Mother of God
With moonlight at its feet
Like a saucer of milk
Set out for a cat to find
As it sneaks in at dawn.
The flames on her candles
Growing unsteady
As its steps draw close,
The saints over the altar
With their eyes open wide
Like children seeing a ghost.

THE MASQUE

A bit of light from the setting sun,
Lingered on in your wineglass,
As you sat on your front steps
After the last guest had departed,
Watching the darkness come,
The first firefly set out tipsily
Over the lawn carrying a lantern
Like a player in a masque miming
Some scene of madness or despair,
The other players still in hiding,
The wind and the leaves providing
The sole musical accompaniment.

MANY A HOLY MAN

Took a turn whispering in his ear
In some quiet hour of the night,
Telling him how much happier
He'd be if he were to desire nothing,

Urging him to stop dwelling
On the many ups and downs in his life—
Some of them still fresh in his mind—
That brought him to this sorry state,

And make peace with everything
That can't be changed,
Understood, or ever properly resolved—
Like God and one's fate,

And devote his remaining days
To minding that inner light
So that it may let him walk without stumbling
As little by little night overtakes him.

THE LIFEBOAT

That cow left alone tonight
Out in the fields
Does it look up at the stars?
How about the cricket
That has just gone silent?
Was it in awe of what it saw?

The night sky loves
Men and women who climb mountains
To confide in its ear.
O the things I'd say to it
If I were to find myself
Alone in a lifeboat at sea.

PAST THE CEMETARY

It's nice sitting here in the shade
At our small outdoor table
Facing a row of brownstones
In the late afternoon sunlight
Under a cloudless summer sky.

Together with its daily horrors,
Life doles out these small pleasures:
A platter of raw oysters on ice,
A ripe lemon sliced in half,
And a glass of chilled white wine.

If the couple holding hands at the next table
Are now in a hurry to leave,
Let them go ahead.
We'll linger over this bottle
And then go looking for a bed ourselves.

STAR ATLAS

The madness of it, Miss Dickinson!
Then the dawning suspicion—
We are here alone ventriloquizing
For the one we call God.

Just to be sure, I lifted my eyes
From the star atlas to the night sky
And found one tiny star in it
Above a field covered in snow.

One more mystery for some boy
To ponder as he closes his schoolbook,
Sleepy boy chewing a thumb
As he rests his head on a table.

His tomorrow's classroom empty;
Its huge blackboard wiped clean.
Just a low voice talking on TV
In the janitor's quarters down the hall.

A quick tour by weather satellite
Of the bleak and desolate northern regions
Of our planet, predicting dropping
Temperatures and a blizzard or two

Someplace out there hard to imagine,
Like these photos of distant nebulae—
Blurry remains where portraits of old gods
Once hung hiding the horror from us.

The once popular sitcom everyone watched
Recounting their furies and squabbles
Regarding the fate of their terrestrial subjects,
Has been canceled, some say indefinitely.

The huge cast joining the line of the unemployed
Winding around the globe, stamping
Their feet and blowing on their hands
To keep warm as the long freeze sets in.

NIGHT OWLS

Addicts of introspection,
Inmates of inner prisons
Drawn and quartered
Between body and soul,

Eyeballing time and eternity,
Making burglar's tools
Out of your ecstatic visions
To pick the lock of their mystery.

Scribblers of briefs and writs
Against a dissembling God.
Mad dogs of mystic love
On your way to the pound.

Fellow sufferers, wretches like me
And you pretty ladies too,
Each nailed to her own cross,
Let's all get some shut-eye if we can.

AT TENDER MERCY

O lone streetlight,
Trying to shed
What light you can
On a spider repairing his web
This autumn night,
Stay with me,
As I push further and further
Into the dark.

CHARLES SIMIC is a poet, essayist, and translator. He was born in Yugoslavia in 1938 and immigrated to the United States in 1954. His first poems were published in 1959, when he was twenty-one. In 1961 he was drafted into the U.S. Army, and in 1966 he earned his bachelor's degree from New York University while working during the day to cover the costs of tuition. Since 1967, he has published twenty books of his own poetry, seven books of essays, a memoir, and numerous books of translations of Serbian, Croatian, and Slovenian poetry, for which he has received many literary awards, including the Pulitzer Prize, the Griffin Prize, the MacArthur Fellowship, and the Wallace Stevens Award. His *New and Selected Poems (1962–2012)* was published in 2013 and *The Lunatic* was published in 2015. Simic is a frequent contributor to the *New York Review of Books* and in 2007 he was chosen as poet laureate of the United States. He is emeritus professor of the University of New Hampshire, where he has taught since 1973.